WOODLANDS
AROUND THE WORLD

WOODLANDS
AROUND THE WORLD
BY CORINNE J. NADEN

◄— A FIRST BOOK —►

FRANKLIN WATTS, INC.
NEW YORK 1973

To Mary Lee Graeme
and the ten million leaves on her lawn.

Photographs courtesy of: Australian News & Information Bureau: 7; Trans World Airline: 30; Union Pacific Railroad: 10, 58; United Nations: 26, 27, 69; U.S. Forest Service: 22, 29, 40, 60; U.S. Forest Service photographers: James L. Averell, 38 (top); Paul S. Carter, 5 (bottom); Ray S. Cragin, 55; David T. Funk, 38 (bottom); P. Freeman Heim, 9; Richard W. Mosher, 5 (top); Bluford W. Muir, 48; H. H. Muntz, 64; Oliver B. Noonan, 52; F. G. Plummer, 44; Leland J. Prater, 47, 53; W. H. Shaffer, 42; H. L. Shantz, 36; Harry Sperling, 62; A. G. Varela, 14.

Cover design by One + One Studio
Maps and diagrams by Thomas R. Funderburk

Library of Congress Cataloging in Publication Data

Naden, Corinne J
    Woodlands around the world.

    (A First book)
    SUMMARY: Discusses the formation, characteristics, and ecology of trees and forests emphasizing conservation efforts of the United States. Also lists the 153 National Forests and the major tree types in this country.
    Bibliography: p.
    1. Forests and forestry–Juvenile literature. 2. Forests and forestry–United States — Juvenile literature. 3. Trees–Juvenile literature.

[1. Forests and forestry. 2. Trees] I. Title.
SD376.N3   574.5'264   72-12712
ISBN 0-531-00802-9

CONTENTS

77 Cy 100

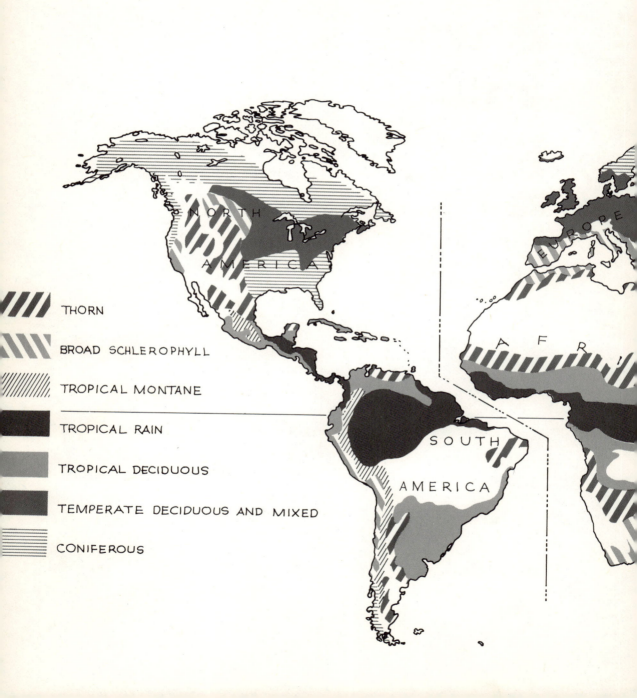

THORN

BROAD SCHLEROPHYLL

TROPICAL MONTANE

TROPICAL RAIN

TROPICAL DECIDUOUS

TEMPERATE DECIDUOUS AND MIXED

CONIFEROUS

NORTH AMERICA

SOUTH AMERICA

EUROPE

AFRICA

The forested areas of the world.

WHAT ARE WOODLANDS?

The planet earth contains about 50 million square miles of land. Long ago most of it was covered by woodlands, or forests. A *forest* is a growth of trees and shrubs, usually extending over a large area.

Forests have been on earth for a very long time. About 200 million years ago, plants that were much like today's kinds of trees began to appear. Even before that — perhaps 300 million years ago — forests of scale trees, a kind of giant club moss, grew in warm, moist lowland areas. The club moss is not a true moss. Modern club mosses are small, but are related to the larger, extinct plants.

By about 100 million years ago, these wooded areas had evolved into forests that looked a good deal like those seen today. In fact, no new major tree groups have appeared on earth since that time.

Over millions of years, the earth has gone through many changes in climate. One such change occurred about 65 million years ago, when large parts of the planet became warm and moist. Tropical plants began to push north, to what is now Canada in North America and the British Isles in Europe. When the climate changed again, some 15 million years ago, and became much drier, the forests retreated toward the equator.

Another great change in climate happened during the Ice Age, when glaciers covered a large part of northern Asia, Europe, and North America. The climate became very cold. When the last glacier retreated, some 10,000 years ago, about half of the world's land was forested.

Today woodlands cover less than one-third of the earth's surface. They grow widely throughout the temperate regions of the Northern Hemisphere, and in various parts of the Southern Hemisphere. (See the map on page 2.)

The parts of the earth not naturally covered by forests are the *grasslands*, level regions with a natural covering of grasses, found in both hemispheres; the *deserts*, also in both hemispheres; the flat treeless Arctic area known as the *tundra;* and the *ice caps* of Canada, Greenland, and the Antarctic.

In many parts of the world, a transition area exists between forested and nonforested regions. Tall prairie grasses and some trees may grow there.

Woodlands have always been important to man. Trees provide wood for fuel and lumber for building things, as well as for many important products. Paper, for instance, is made from wood fiber.

Woodlands are also important simply because they are some of the most beautiful spots in the world. Each year millions of Americans spend vacation and other leisure time in national forests all over the country.

There is still another reason that forests are important to us. Plants, including trees, furnish the world's oxygen.

Animal life, including man, breathes in oxygen from the air and gives off carbon dioxide, a colorless, odorless gas. More than 10 percent of carbon dioxide in the air in a given area can cause unconsciousness. Eventually, it can cause death from lack of oxygen.

On the other hand, plant life consumes carbon dioxide and puts oxygen into the air. This process is called *photosynthesis*.

Photosynthesis works in this way: Using the energy that comes from sunlight, green plants take carbon dioxide from the air and water from the soil to make sugar. Sugar is a plant's basic food. The water absorbed by the plant is changed into atoms of oxygen and hydrogen. *Chlorophyll*, the green substance in plant leaves, brings about this chemical change. Some of the oxygen and hydrogen atoms join to form water once again, which the plant stores. The other hydrogen atoms join with the carbon dioxide to form glucose, an important sugar in all living things. The remaining oxygen is not used by the plant. It escapes into the air.

Plant and animal life work together to keep the air livable. Without plants, there would be no oxygen after a time.

Forests play an important part in this balance between carbon dioxide and oxygen in the air. In one year, an acre of healthy young trees can produce four tons of new wood, consume about six tons of carbon dioxide, and give off four tons of fresh oxygen. That makes a healthy forest just about the best pollution fighter we have!

The world's forests can be put into two main categories: those containing mostly *deciduous* (de-*sid*-u-us), also called hardwood, trees, and those containing mostly *conifers* (*kon*-e-furs), also called softwoods. The elm, oak, and maple are examples of deciduous trees. The pine, spruce, and hemlock are conifers.

Most deciduous trees have broad leaves, which they shed each year. (The name deciduous comes from a Latin word that means "to fall off.") However, some broadleaf trees, such as the palm tree, do not shed their leaves each year.

4

A forest of conifers in Colorado.

A maple tree rising above the deciduous forest in North Carolina.

Conifers have needlelike leaves, and most of them bear their seeds in cones. (The name conifer means "cone bearer.") Coniferous trees, which make up about 30 percent of the world's forests, are usually evergreen. As a conifer's needlelike leaves are falling off, new ones are growing, so the tree stays green. However, there are some exceptions. The larch is a conifer that does shed all its leaves each year.

The climate largely determines the type of forest. Broadleaf trees grow well in warm, moist regions, while the needle-leafed trees thrive in dry, cool areas. There are large stretches of coniferous forests in the more northern regions of the Northern Hemisphere, as well as in the mountain regions of the Southern Hemisphere. Forests in tropical areas are usually dense with broadleafs. In regions where cool-dry climate meets warm-moist climate, the forests may be a combination of both types of trees.

There are seven principal kinds of forests: thorn; broad sclerophyll (hard-leaved) woodland; tropical montane; tropical rain; tropical deciduous; temperate deciduous and mixed; and coniferous.

Thorn forests are found in northern Australia, parts of South America, India, and Mexico. Their small deciduous trees thrive in the hot, dry climates. Rainfall is usually no higher than 25 inches yearly. Large shrubs such as mesquite and acacia also grow there. This is a transitional area between the true deciduous forest and the desert.

Broad sclerophyll (hard-leaved) woodlands are located in Chile, California, around the Mediterranean Sea, in southern Australia, and in South Africa. The annual rainfall in these areas may be 30 inches. The summers are dry and hot, and the winters wet and mild. These forests mostly contain small ever-

An area of thorn forest in central Australia.

6

A tropical rain palm forest in Puerto Rico.

green trees and shrubs. Olive trees grow in the Mediterranean area and eucalyptus trees, the favorite of the koala bear, in Australia.

Africa, Asia, and Central and South America contain *tropical montane* forests. Temperatures may reach 75 degrees, and the rainfall is usually between 40 and 80 inches. Broadleaf evergreen trees grow there.

Tropical rain forests are found in Central and South America, central and western Africa, India, Asia, and Australia. The rainfall is high — up to 200 inches — and the temperature is warm most of the year. These forests usually contain tall, broadleaf, evergreen trees, bamboos (huge, fast-growing grasses), and different kinds of ferns and mosses.

The *tropical deciduous* forest contains broadleaf trees that are usually smaller than those found in rain forests. The temperature is about the same as in the rain forest, but the rainfall is less — up to 100 inches. Teak grows in these forests in southeastern Asia. Other tropical deciduous forests are located in Central and South America, Asia, and Africa.

Temperate deciduous and mixed forests occur in the eastern United States, Europe, and Asia. Although they may contain some conifers, the trees are mostly hardwoods, such as walnut, maple, and oak. The summers are hot, the winters cold, and the rainfall — from 30 to 60 inches — falls fairly evenly throughout the year.

Coniferous forests are spread widely across the temperate regions of the Northern Hemisphere. The U.S.S.R. has 45 percent of the world's coniferous forests; North America has 36 percent. These forests usually contain types of fir, pine, and spruce trees. Douglas fir and Sitka spruce thrive along the coastlands of the Pacific Ocean, and huge redwoods grow in a narrow fog belt in northern California. In the most northern regions, coniferous trees grow in very cold winters and short, cool summers.

The woodlands of the eastern United States and southern Canada experience probably the greatest seasonal changes of any forests in the world. Lying in the so-called Temperate Zone, these areas go through great extremes of climate, from bitter icy winters to tropical-like summers. As a result, the for-

Autumn colors the leaves in this Utah forest of mixed deciduous and coniferous trees.

ests change greatly, too, even though these changes may seem only natural — as indeed they are — to the people who live nearby.

Spring comes to an eastern woodland with small bright flowers that make a carpet for the forest floor. Birds return from their winter journeys to snatch at the earthworms tunneling up from below ground. Cottontail rabbits and fluffy wood ducks are born into the forest world. Trees, from the lowest shrub to the highest oak, spread their leaves in many shades of green over the forest. The oak is the last to gain its leaves. When it does, summer has come to the forest.

In the summer heat, thousands of insects fill the eastern forests with noise. All through the summer days, they are busy attacking the tree leaves. By the end of summer hardly a leaf will be left untouched. Mushrooms sprout at the bases of trees. Animals search for food among the lush plant growth. The forest is shady under its canopy of green.

Here and there a leaf flutters to the ground as autumn approaches. Trees turn their leaves to blazing reds and golds and scatter hickory nuts and acorns across the forest floor. They are quickly picked up and eaten or stored by the woodland animals. Birds begin to leave the forest for the south. Chipmunks and black snakes get ready to curl up into balls to sleep through the winter. Turtles and frogs settle into the mud of their pools. The whole pace of forest life begins to quiet and slow down.

In winter, snow covers sleeping animals and the bare branches of the trees. All seems quiet. The forest is waiting for spring.

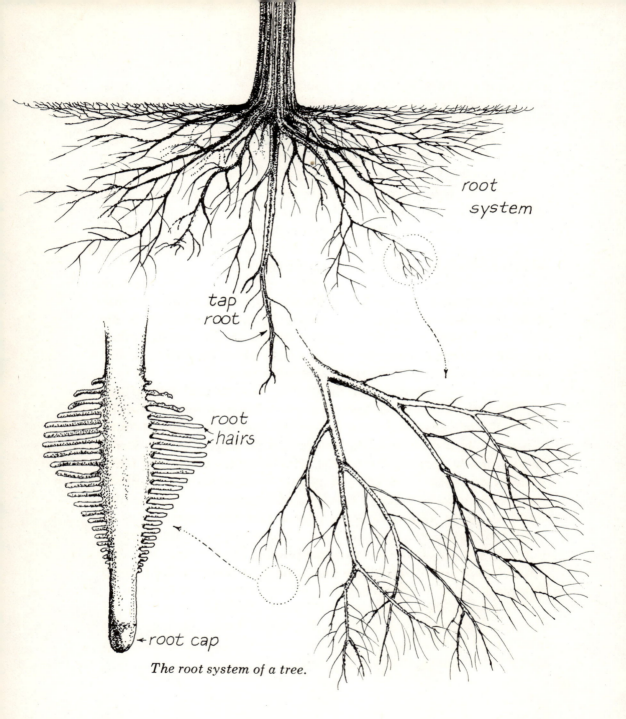

root
system

tap
root

root
hairs

root cap

The root system of a tree.

THE LIVING TREE

A tree is a plant — woody, seed-bearing, perennial (living for more than one season), and usually large and long-lived. In fact, the largest and oldest living thing in the world today is a tree — larger than a whale, larger than anything alive. Redwood trees on the West Coast have reached over 360 feet tall. One of California's giant sequoias, named General Grant, is 267.4 feet tall, over 40 feet in diameter, and still growing. It contains enough wood to build 50 six-room houses! General Grant is thought to be 3,500 years old. Bristlecone pines, found mainly in the White Mountains of California, are even older, perhaps as much as 4,600 years old. Such trees are in great contrast to a 20-foot-high dogwood, or a gray birch, which lives about 40 years. But they are all trees just the same.

Every tree, no matter what kind, has the same basic parts — roots, trunk, branches, and leaves.

A tree's *root system* does two things: it anchors the tree to the ground and it absorbs water and minerals from the soil.

A root system may be very large. Spreading out in all directions beneath the ground, the roots keep the tree from falling over. A tree may have a *taproot* — a long main root with many other roots growing from it.

13

The pillar roots of a banyan tree.

Trees need water. The leaves of a tree can give off hundreds of gallons of water on a hot day. The stringlike tips of a tree's roots churn through the soil in a kind of corkscrew motion, drinking in great amounts of water and minerals. Cell by cell, the water and minerals are passed upward — through the roots, through the trunk, through the branches, to the leaves.

Root tips are delicate but strong. Each tip wears a protective cap, somewhat like a thimble. Behind the cap are thousands of white root hairs, each with a single cell. These cells take in water as they grip the soil. Root hairs die after a few days, and new ones grow. The root system branches and rebranches in its never-ending search for water.

Some trees also have roots on the surface. The bald cypress, which thrives in swampy areas, grows "knees" on its roots above the water to get air. The strangler fig sends its roots around a host tree and chokes the host to death. Roots of other trees sprout from the trunk and enter the ground, becoming "extra trunks." One banyan tree in Calcutta, India, had over 200 extra trunks, called *pillar roots*. They help to support the tree's far-spreading branches.

Tree roots benefit the tree, but they also are an aid to the soil. Spreading out underground, the roots help to hold the soil in place, preventing it from being washed away by rain or blown away by wind.

As tree roots support the trunk, so the tree trunk supports the branches and leaves. A tree may have one single trunk rising all the way to the top. The branches growing from it get shorter as they go up. Or a tree may have a trunk that divides and redivides into branches. The white pine is an example of a single trunk. The trunk of the American elm is divided.

The outside, visible layer of a tree trunk is called the *outer bark*. Smooth in young trees, the bark stretches as the trunk grows thicker. As it stretches it may split or crack in various ways. These typical cracks help to distinguish one kind of tree from another. Beech tree bark stretches easily and smoothly, while the bark of the sycamore stretches very little. Instead, it splits and flakes off the tree in big patches, giving the sycamore a splotchy look. The bark of the white birch peels off in very

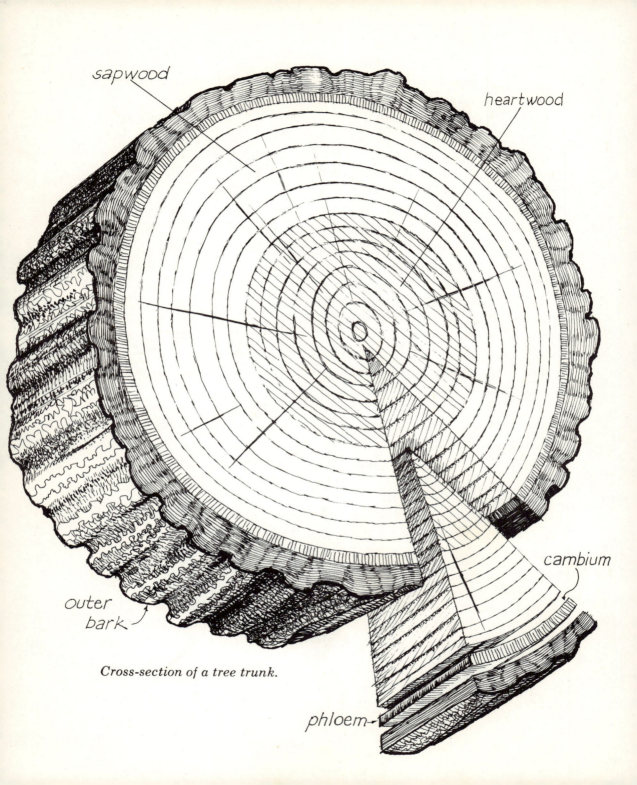

sapwood

heartwood

cambium

outer
bark

phloem

Cross-section of a tree trunk.

thin strips. The bark of the ponderosa pine is black until the tree is about 100 years old. Then the bark turns a reddish brown color. Some barks are very thin. But the tough bark of the redwood may be a foot thick. The outer bark protects the tree from rain, heat and cold, and insects and disease.

Just inside the outer bark is the inner bark, called *phloem* (floem). It carries food from the leaves to the roots. When it dies, it becomes part of the outer bark.

Next to the bark layers is a thin, living-tissue layer called *cambium*. Each year the cambium divides into a new layer of phloem on one side and a new layer of sapwood on the other.

The *sapwood* layer of a tree trunk carries sap — water and dissolved minerals — throughout the tree. In the spring, when the tree has lots of water, the cambium builds large, light-colored cells. In the fall, when the tree has less water, the cambium builds smaller cells with thicker walls. They look darker in color than the cells created in spring. These light and dark circles of sapwood, taken together, make an *annual ring*. Added to each year by the cambium, they tell the age of a tree.

In 1901 Andrew E. Douglass of the Lowell Observatory in Arizona discovered that age could be determined by counting the sapwood circles in a cross section of a tree. Ten sapwood circles meant the tree was ten years old. One hundred circles meant 100 years.

It is possible that in a very dry period a tree may not grow very much. Therefore, the cambium layer may not build a complete new sapwood circle. Or, during a long dry spell, the annual rings may be very narrow. Broad, evenly spaced rings show that the tree grew with plenty of light and water.

17

The center of a tree trunk is dark dead tissue called *heart-wood*. It is formed when the older water-carrying tubes of the sapwood are no longer needed. They harden and become clogged with gums and resins. The heartwood is the core of the tree, giving it strength and support.

Depending upon the kind of tree, branches grow out from the trunk in different ways. A sugar maple usually looks as though someone has deliberately trimmed its branches into a near-perfect oval. The slender branches of a weeping willow droop to the ground. The branches of an eastern hemlock grow smaller and smaller toward the top, giving the tree a tri-angular shape.

A tree's branches hold its leaves. And each tree leaf is a truly remarkable and busy little factory, manufacturing the tree's food by photosynthesis.

In the fall, photosynthesis slows down as the tree gets ready for winter. The green chlorophyll in the leaves of decidu-ous trees begins to waste away. Yellow and red pigments start to show in the leaves as the tree takes on its bright autumn coloring. Finally, the tree sheds its leaves.

Leaves come in all sizes and shapes. Pine needles are long and thin. The leaf of the sweet gum tree is star-shaped. The weeping willow leaf looks like a feather. The flowering dog-wood has an oval-shaped leaf with smooth edges.

Leaves grow on branches either opposite each other, like the maple tree, or alternately, like the elm. Some leaves are called *simple leaves* because they are all in one piece. Maple and white poplar leaves are simple. The white ash tree has *compound leaves*. Each leaf is divided into separate leaflets.

Veins in the leaves carry sap. If the leaf has one center vein with smaller veins branching off, it is called *pinnate* — having the shape of a feather. The oak tree has pinnate leaves.

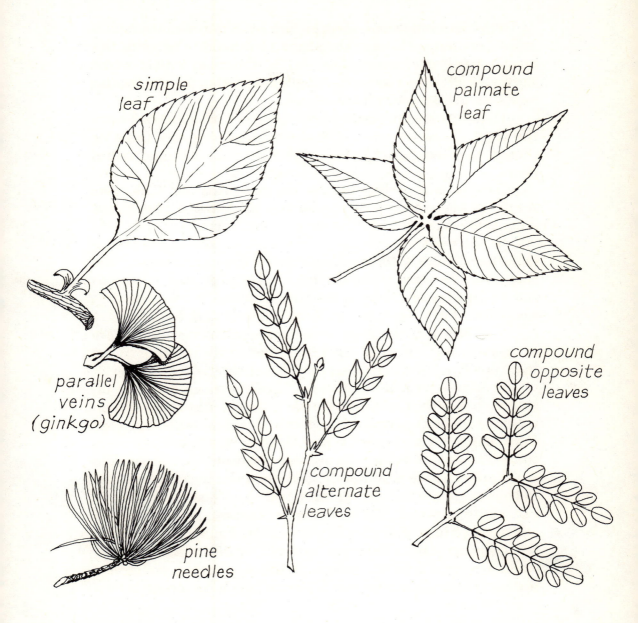

*simple
leaf*

*compound
palmate
leaf*

*parallel
veins
(ginkgo)*

*compound
opposite
leaves*

*pine
needles*

*compound
alternate
leaves*

If the veins branch out through the leaf from the stem, it is called *palmate* — having the shape of a hand. The sycamore tree has palmate leaves. The leaf of the ginkgo tree, which grows mainly in China and Japan, is unusual. It has *parallel* veins, as the drawing shows.

Trees grow from seeds. Seeds develop from a tree's flowers or cones. There are two types of seeds: *angiosperm*, meaning "seeds in a container," and *gymnosperm*, meaning "naked seeds."

The seeds of coniferous trees are gymnosperms. They have no protective covering. A conifer has male and female cones. The male cone produces pollen — tiny sperm cells. In the spring the pollen is carried by the wind to the larger female cone. Seeds form in the cone. When the cone ripens, which may take years in some trees, the cone splits open and the seeds fall to the ground. All conifers are pollinated by wind, and so are some hardwood trees, such as the ash and oak.

The seeds of flowering trees are angiosperms. They are enclosed in a covering of some type. Pollen is carried from the male flower, or the male part of a flower, to the female flower, or the female part of the flower. (The magnolia tree, for instance, has both male and female parts in the same flower. Other trees have separate male and female flowers.) A seed forms in the female flower. When the seed is ripe, it drifts away to the ground. If conditions are right, a new tree will grow.

Flowering trees do not depend upon the wind for pollination. Their flowers attract animals and insects, such as the bee. Flitting from flower to flower, the bee carries and deposits the pollen, thus fertilizing the female flower. Fruit trees, such as the apple, may have their seeds spread by deer and other animals. The deer eats the fruit and the seed passes unharmed through its digestive tract to be deposited on the ground.

20

Different trees produce seeds at different times. A peach tree will produce its first seeds when it is five years old, but an oak will not produce its first seeds until it is 50. The sequoia may wait for about 250 years, which isn't very long for a tree that may live to be over 3,000.

A tree may live for many years or many centuries. But it may also be destroyed before its life span is reached. Forest fires kill trees and men cut them down. A tree has other enemies, too.

Insects are tree destroyers. Aphids draw juice from tree leaves. The liquid they secrete clogs the pores of plants and kills them. The 17-year locust slits open a twig and deposits its eggs, badly damaging the branch. When the eggs hatch, the young locusts fall to the ground and burrow beneath the soil, sucking juices from the tree roots. Scale insects cover a tree with scales and choke it.

One of the most destructive of a tree's enemies is the leaf-cutting ant. These pests can strip a tree bare in a single day. They bite leaves into pieces and carry them off to the nest in their strong jaws. In the nest the leaves are chewed into pulp and used as fertilizer to grow a fungus, which is the ants' food.

Caterpillars are another tree enemy. An almost endless variety of these creatures constantly attack trees. Woolly, spotted, striped, and spiny caterpillars feast away on elm, apple, oak, and all kinds of trees, sometimes stripping a forest bare for miles.

Another enemy of trees is disease. Blight is the general term for any disease that attacks plant tissue. Tree leaves are most affected by blight. They yellow, turn brown, and dry up. Believed to be caused by bacteria, blight can be controlled in some cases with fungicides, but once started blight is often difficult to stop.

21

In the early twentieth century, blight affected the American chestnut tree. As a result, this tree species has been very nearly wiped out. Today Dutch elm disease is attacking large parts of the United States, especially in the Midwest, causing destruction of these trees. In the early 1940's a disease began to attack the oak tree. Today it is present in nearly all of the midwestern states and as far east as Pennsylvania and North Carolina. There is no cure for the disease. Once having attacked an oak tree, the fungus may kill it within a few weeks, or in one season at the most.

A tree may also simply die of old age. At 40, a gray birch is old, but 40 is a young age to the sugar maple, which may reach 500. When a tree is old, its growing process slows down. It cannot easily bring water and food to the leaves and roots. The lack of food and water causes branches to die and break off. The bark starts to scale. Finally, the tree becomes so weak that a strong wind will blow it over, or it will just fall by itself.

Even a dead tree is useful. It becomes part of the debris of the forest floor. Softened by water and fungus growths, it is attacked by earthworms, ants, and other creatures. Fungi — in the form of mushrooms and toadstools — make even the tree bark eatable for animals.

The American Forestry Association keeps a list of record trees — the biggest in each species. (Anyone who discovers a record tree in the United States should send the information to the association's headquarters in Washington, D.C.) The tallest tree may not necessarily be the biggest, however. Champions are determined by adding the height in feet; one-quarter of the crown spread — how far the tree top branches out — in feet; and the circumference of the tree in inches. (Circumference is measured 4½ feet up the trunk.)

Fir trees killed by Balsam woolly aphids.

Champion Trees in the United States

Tree Type	Circumference	Height	Spread	Location
Ash, White	22' 3"	80'	82'	Glen Mills, Pa.
Beech, American	15' 2"	106'	106'	Cumberstone, Md.
Birch, Paper	10' 11"	96'	93'	Williamsburg, Mich.
Chestnut, American	15' 17½"	90'	64'	Oregon City, Oreg.
Cypress, Arizona	17' 5"	102'	38'	Coronado National Forest, Ariz.
Dogwood, Flowering	5' 4"	30'	42'	near Oriole, Md.
Douglas Fir	53' 4"	221'	61'	Olympic National Park, Wash.
Elm, American or White	24' 7"	160'	147'	near Trigonia, Tenn.
Hickory, Shellbark	12' 3"	115'	90'	French Lick, Ind.
Holly, American	13' 4"	53'	61'	near Hardin, Tex.
Larch, Eastern	11' 5"	60'	60'	Chaplin, Conn.
Maple, Sugar	19' 9"	116'	75'	Garrett County, Md.
Oak, Black	22' 3"	125'	85'	Warrensville Heights, Ohio
Oak, Live	35'	78'	168'	near Hahnville, La.
Pine, Ponderosa	21' 6"	223'	66'	Sierra National Forest, Calif.
Pine, Shortleaf	10' 7"	146'	60'	Morganton, N.C.
Pine, Western White	21' 3"	219'	36'	near Elk River, Idaho
Redwood, Coast	65' 9"	361'	—	Redwood Highway, Calif.
Sequoia, Giant	101' 6" (at base)	272'	90'	Sequoia National Park, Calif.
Spruce, Engelmann	22'	179'	35'	Olympic National Park, Wash.
Spruce, Sitka	41' 8"	214'	50'	Olympic National Park, Wash.
Tupelo, Black	16' 1"	130'	65'	Noxubee National Wildlife Refuge, Miss.
Walnut, Eastern Black	20' 3"	108'	128'	Anne Arundel County, Md.
Willow, Black	26' 1"	85'	79'	Traverse City, Mich.

WOODLANDS AROUND THE WORLD

Forests, in one or more of the seven main types, cover parts of all the continents in the world, with the exception of Antarctica. (The fifth largest continent, Antarctica is a snow-covered land where only the lowest forms of plant life exist.) But many of the natural wooded areas, especially in Europe, have long been cleared for agriculture and other uses. Today, about 30 percent of Europe is forested. Asia has nearly 20 percent of its land in forest; Africa, about 25 percent; South America, some 50 percent; and Australia, only about 7 percent.

Africa

Covering over 11 million square miles, Africa is the second largest (after Asia) of the world's continents. It is a land of deserts, grasslands, and tropical forests.

The rain forest occurs where the climate is warm and the rainfall is plentiful. In Africa the main rain forest areas are the southwestern coast and the Congo Basin. There is also quite a large area of rain forest in the southeast.

The evergreen rain forest is dense, often keeping sunlight from reaching the forest floor. Many commercially important trees come from these woodlands, such as ebony, mahogany, teak, and oil palm.

The thick mountain forest in the Sudan is edged here with the terraces of a tree nursery.

In drier areas there are patches of semideciduous forest. Mangrove trees grow on both the east and west coásts. The bark of the mangrove is commercially important because it is used for tanning.

In the Ituri (a tributary of the Congo River) rain forest live the BaMbuti Pygmies, a primitive, nomadic people who call themselves "children of the forest." Usually no taller than four feet eight inches, the Pygmies depend upon the rain forest for their daily needs. Their homes are made from young trees, bent over and covered with huge leaves. They raise no food animals and must obtain their meat by hunting, which they do with bow and poisoned arrow. Twenty or more families may take part in the hunt, beating the bushes to frighten the game into long nets made of tree vines.

The BaMbuti women also gather nuts, fruits, and mushrooms. When the supply is gone or game is no longer plentiful, the Pygmies move on to a new home in the forest.

26

A woodland area in Pakistan. Much of the country's forests have been destroyed by man.

Another dweller in some parts of the rain forest is the African gorilla. Rather clumsy tree climbers, gorillas live in low trees or on the ground. Although fierce-looking, these huge animals are actually shy and even-tempered.

Other animals that make their homes in the rain forest are chimpanzees, antelopes, and many types of monkeys. Elephants live in both forest and grassland areas. The forest also shelters snakes, such as the poisonous cobra, and many insects.

Asia

The world's largest continent covers over 17 million square miles. Most of this huge area is filled with mountains, deserts, and plains. The main wooded areas are the tropical forests of India and countries in the southeast and huge stretches of coniferous forest, called *taiga* (*tie*-ga), in the north. Mixed and tropical thorn forests are also scattered about the continent.

Taiga is a Russian word. This forest of mostly spruce and fir trees is a generally open, rather than dense, woodland. There are, however, dense stands of trees, especially around the rivers in the more southern regions of the taiga. In the Siberian taiga the main conifer is the larch, a needle-leafed tree that annually sheds its leaves.

From the tropical rain forests of Asia come teak and sandalwood trees, as well as palm trees such as the coconut and wild date.

Reindeer and moose roam the northern Asian lands and many kinds of monkeys are found in the tropical forests from Japan to India. But larger mammals, such as the Bengal tiger, are unusual.

Australia

Australia's forests are found along the coastal areas. This smallest continent is an island, covering less than three million square miles.

Because Australia has been so long separated from the other land masses, its plant and animal life are unique. A prominent tree is the eucalyptus, of which there are 600 known species. These trees supply valuable hardwood timber.

Rain forests in the province of Queensland, in the northeastern part of the continent, are preserved in national parks. A conifer called bunya-bunya is found there. Another valuable conifer is the cypress pine in the western plains.

The best known of Australia's animals are its marsupials, mammals with pouches to carry their young. The kangaroo is a marsupial, and so is the koala. The most unique of the continent's animals are the monotremes. Like other mammals they are warm-blooded and they feed their young with mother's milk.

Eucalyptus tree grove.

But unlike other mammals, they lay eggs from which the young hatch. There are only two monotremes in the world, the echidna, an anteater, and the platypus, an aquatic animal. The platypus is found only in Australia.

Europe

This second smallest continent has 25 percent of the world's population and 8 percent of its land, or about 3,700,000 square miles. Much of its original forest land has been cleared,

although there are still vast wooded areas in the larger mountain ranges. The coniferous forests in the north contain pines, spruces, and firs. Most of Europe's remaining woodlands are temperate deciduous and mixed forests.

There are a number of well-known forests in Europe, such as the Bohemian Forest of Czechoslovakia, the Ardennes in France, and the Black Forest in the West German province of Baden-Württemberg. The Black Forest covers an area 100 miles long and from 10 to 30 miles wide, with the Rhine River as its southern and western boundary. The dark color of its fir trees gives the forest its name, although it also contains beech and oak trees. Besides being a popular winter resort, the Black Forest is an important source of timber and pulpwood for paper products.

South America

Fourth largest of the seven continents, South America covers nearly seven million square miles. Much of the continent lies below the equator. In such a huge area, there are many contrasts, ranging from the Andes Mountains, running from Colombia in the north to the southern tip of Chile, to the flat, treeless plain of Argentina, known as the pampa.

About 50 percent of South America is forested, mainly some type of tropical forest. There are also small areas of coniferous forests in southern Chile and some pine and broadleaf forests in southern Brazil.

South America's tropical forests fall into three groups: tropical scrub or thorn; tropical semideciduous; and tropical rain forest, also called selva.

The Black Forest of Germany.

Tropical rain forest bordered by a river in the Guiana countries.

The *tropical scrub* or *thorn* forest is the driest of the three groups. This type is found mainly in a plains area called the Gran Chaco, in Argentina, Paraguay, and Bolivia. The coastal lowland of Colombia also contains scrub or thorn forests. To make up for the relative dryness, the trees have small leaves and thick bark as protection against drought.

The *tropical semideciduous* forest is scattered around the continent, in southeast Bolivia, eastern and southern Brazil, northeast Venezuela, and other small areas. Some of the trees in these forests remain green; others shed their leaves each year. Temperatures are usually high, and the rainfall is greater than in the scrub or thorn forest.

The *selva* forest has the highest temperatures and rainfall — in places over 100 inches a year — of the three groups. It is the largest tropical rain forest in the world, covering the Amazon Basin and extending into the Brazilian highlands and the Guiana countries. It is also found in Ecuador and Colombia.

This rain forest of broadleaf evergreens is so thick that sunlight rarely touches the forest floor. As a result, there is very little undergrowth. A nearly impassable jungle, the selva provides the wood of mahogany and ebony trees, as well as rubber and Brazil-nut trees.

The Guaica Indians are people of the rain forest. They live around the headwaters of the Orinoco River. A primitive people who do not know how to make metal tools or build canoes, the Guaicas grow cotton and tobacco and have recently learned to cultivate sweet potatoes. These Indians were driven into the forest many years ago.

Although primitive, the Guaicas are a little more advanced than the Pygmies. They know how to make fire by friction. They weave baskets and hunt with long bows of palm wood. When going out on a hunt, the men paint themselves with patterns to bring good luck. Home to the Guaica family is a kind of lean-to built against a huge tree in the rain forest.

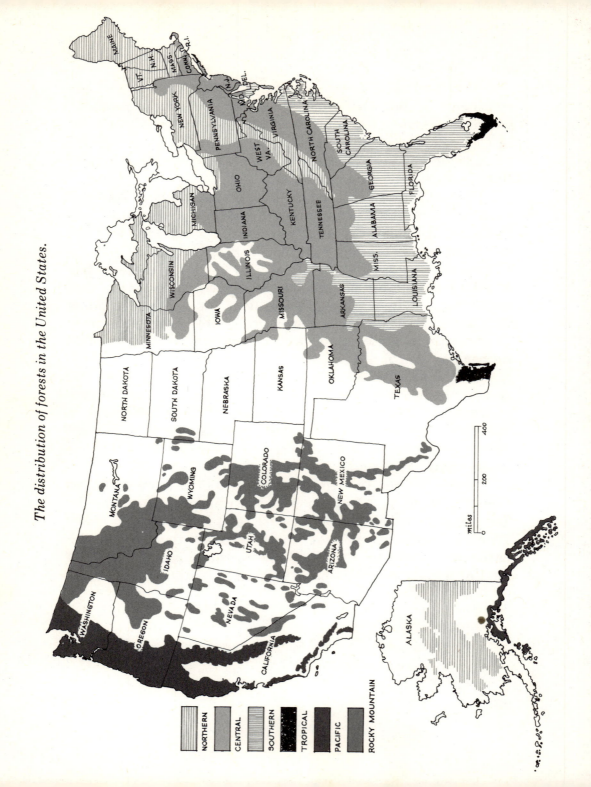

The distribution of forests in the United States.

NORTHERN
CENTRAL
SOUTHERN
TROPICAL
PACIFIC
ROCKY MOUNTAIN

WOODLANDS IN THE UNITED STATES

The continent of North America is very large — the third largest of the seven continents, after Asia and Africa. It covers about nine million square miles, or nearly 15 percent of the earth's land surface. It has different kinds of climate and contains many different kinds of soil. Therefore, it also contains a great variety of plant life. Nearly 1,200 kinds of trees grow in North America. About 40 percent of the continent's total land area is woodland.

Left in its natural state, the United States would be largely covered by woodlands. The main nonforested areas are the Great Plains, running north and south nearly in the middle of the country; the desert and mountain regions of the West; and about half the state of Alaska. (See the map on page 34.) The most heavily forested of the 50 states is Maine, with 89.7 percent of its land covered by trees. New Hampshire is second with 88.7 percent. The least forested state is North Dakota. Only 1 percent of its territory is forest land.

There are less than 800 million acres of actual forest land in the United States today. Over 500 million acres are what is called the commercial forest. This is the land that Americans use for recreation and that provides the material for the thousands of wood products we need. Private individuals own more than 300 million acres of the commercial forest; the govern-

The Northern Forest in Alaska.

ment, both state and federal, owns over 140 million acres; and the forest products industry owns about 66 million acres.

The remaining forest land in the United States — less than 300 million acres — is either not suited for growing commercial timber or it is set aside as wilderness areas or parks.

Forests in the United States are divided into six major regions: Northern, Central, Southern, Tropical, Rocky Mountain, and Pacific.

The *Northern Forest* spreads some 4,000 miles from Alaska across Canada, to the northern midwest and eastern states, and down into the Appalachian area. This is largely a coniferous forest, the home of the black spruce in the far north, the balsam fir, eastern hemlock, northern white cedar, and eastern white pine.

The wood of the balsam fir is soft and light in color, and is much in demand for making paper. Averaging between 20 and 60 feet tall, the balsam fir is a favorite Christmas tree because of its fragrance and shape. It also keeps its dark-green needles for a long time after being cut.

The white pine supplied much of the lumber needs for the United States in its early growth. The original stand of eastern white pine is said to have been 750 billion board feet of wood. (One board foot measures 12 inches by 12 inches by 1 inch.) It was used for building homes and for making furniture and many other products. When these eastern pine forests were destroyed by overcutting, the loggers moved west. Around the 1850's, Pennsylvania, New York, and Maine were the leading lumber states; 25 years later, Wisconsin, Minnesota, and Michigan had replaced them.

There are deciduous trees in the Northern Forest, too. Yellow birch is probably the most widespread. The American chestnut once grew widely in the Appalachian region. Other kinds of trees found in this forest are walnuts, hickories, and oaks.

The Northern Forest has generally poor soil. Much of the land in the most northern parts is flat, a reminder of the long-ago glaciers that scraped off the hilltops in Canada. The rest of the area is dotted with lakes, rivers, and hills.

The *Central Forest* touches 30 states and covers about 130 million acres. It reaches from New England to Minnesota and as far south as Texas. This is mainly a natural hardwood

A Southern Forest of longleaf pine in Florida.

The Central Forest in Illinois.

forest, although much of the area is now farmland. The soil is so rich in this region that the trees were cut down to grow crops.

About 40 different kinds of trees grow in the Central Forest. The white oak is the only tree that grows throughout the entire area. It has strong durable wood and was once used in building ships and bridges. Today it is used for floors and furniture. Sycamore, sweet gum, and pine are found in the southern states, oaks and hickories in the Midwest, and beech and maple in New England.

The sugar maple provides maple sugar and syrup. From 30 to 40 gallons of sap boil down to one gallon of syrup. The yellow poplar (also called the tulip tree because of its tulip-shaped flowers) is one of the biggest trees in the southeastern United States, and one of the only two species in this tree family. The other grows in China. Despite its name, it is not really a member of the poplar family. The tree belongs to the magnolias, and its soft yellow wood is used to make crates and boxes.

Because the Central Forest largely contains deciduous trees, it is one of the most changeable of woodlands — from lush green in summer, to brilliant reds and golds in fall, to bare branches in winter.

Sweeping across the Southeast is the *Southern Forest*, a land of pine trees — slash, longleaf, shortleaf, and loblolly. It also contains many hardwoods, such as oak, elm, red maple, and cottonwood.

The soil of the Southern Forest is sandy, in which pine trees grow well. At the turn of the century, most of the country's timber came from this region. The longleaf pine was once a main source of timber. Often reaching 100 feet and more, its wood is strong and hard, which makes it desirable in construction. It is also used for floors and railroad ties.

39

The Southern Forest once supplied some two-thirds of the world's rosin and turpentine. It still furnishes crude resin and gum from its pine trees, chiefly the longleaf pine.

The smallest woodland zone in the United States is called the *Tropical Forest*. It is found only at the tip of Florida — containing the Everglades — and in southeastern Texas. Mahogany trees and mangroves grow in this area of near-constant summer. The tangled arching roots of the mangrove rise out of sand and water to make travel through the trees nearly impossible. Although some mangroves grow to a height of about 60 feet, most of the trees are not very large. Other broadleaf trees, such as palms, grow there.

The *Rocky Mountain Forest* is scattered through the West, from the country's northern border to Texas, from Oregon to the tip of Oklahoma. This is a huge area of deserts and mountains and relatively little rainfall. Rain coming from the Pacific is blocked by the Coast and Cascade ranges.

Trees grow on the Rocky Mountains from an altitude of about 5,000 feet above sea level to about 11,500 feet. Past this higher altitude, called the *timber line*, the climate is too severe for normal tree growth. Instead, the land above the timber line is covered with vines, bushes, and ankle-high spruce and fir trees. The topmost peaks have no trees at all.

The main tree species in the Rocky Mountain Forest are the ponderosa pine, the Douglas fir, the western white pine, and Engelmann spruce. The ponderosa pine was named for its great size. It reaches heights of more than 200 feet and may live for over 300 years. An important timber tree, it is used in construction and for wood paneling.

Piñon pine and juniper trees cover acre after acre in the Rocky Mountain Forest. And in the White Mountains of Cali-

A Tropical Forest of 50 foot high mangroves.

Engelmann spruce at the timberline of a Rocky Mountain Forest.

fornia grows the bristlecone pine, said to be the oldest living thing on earth.

For 3,000 miles, from Alaska to California, stretches the spectacular *Pacific Forest*. Its great stands of conifers are like no other in the world. Dense growths of western hemlock, Sitka spruce, and Douglas fir are found in the lush Olympic rain forest of Washington. This forest is the only one of its kind in North America. Fog-covered and wet — it gets up to 150 inches of rain a year — the Olympic rain forest juts into the Pacific Ocean. Its trees are choked with moss, and the forest floor is covered with ferns and rotting trees. The soil is so wet that trees are more easily uprooted there than in a drier woodland.

The Douglas fir is the world's most important timber tree. It accounts for one-fourth of all the timber standing in the United States. Growing mainly in Washington and Oregon, the Douglas fir may reach over 300 feet tall and as much as 17 feet in diameter. It is used in building construction because its wood is strong and easy to work.

The heavy, strong wood of the western hemlock makes it another popular tree for building, as well as for paper making. Sometimes reaching 250 feet in height, the western hemlock may have a trunk that is ten feet thick.

The most spectacular trees in the Pacific Forest are northern California's giant sequoias and coast redwoods, the earth's largest living things. The land, climate, and rainfall have created this unique plant life. Mountain ranges along the coast reach a height of 14,000 feet. Westerly winds push warm, moisture-filled air toward them from the Pacific. When the air reaches the coastline, it quickly hits the mountains. The air rises, cools, and becomes rain or snow. The mountains trap huge quantities of this moisture, producing rain-forest conditions in a temperate zone.

The straight and handsome redwoods grow in a foggy Pacific Coast area about 15 miles wide and 500 miles long. The more rare sequoias, also called simply the big trees of California, are found on the western slope of the Sierra Nevadas and nowhere else in the world. Naturalist John Muir (1838–1914) called them "the noblest of a noble race." These graceful trees with dark, blue green foliage grow at altitudes from about 4,000 to 8,000 feet in some 70 groves, forming a 250-mile-long belt. The Calaveras grove, discovered in 1841, is the most impressive, but the Mariposa grove contains probably the most famous of the sequoias. Called the Wawona, it has a tunnel cut in its base allowing cars to drive through it.

Redwoods and big trees make up the group of conifers called *sequoia*. Known scientifically as *sequoia sempervirens*, the redwoods are the taller of the two, but the big trees, or *sequoia gigantea*, are bigger in girth and they generally live longer. Redwoods can reach about 350 feet and 20 feet in diameter; sequoias average about 275 feet and 25 feet in diameter.

The main reason that these huge conifers live so long is that they have very few enemies. The bark of the giant sequoia may be two feet thick; redwood bark is often one foot thick. Insects do little harm to the bark, which is nearly fireproof. Only under very extreme circumstances can fire penetrate the thick shaggy barks of the older giant trees. Plant diseases rarely attack them, and the roots are so large that it would be practically impossible for the wind to blow them over. That leaves only man as a serious threat.

Most redwoods are cut down when they are from 400 to 800 years old. The wood, from light cherry to dark mahogany in color, is very durable. Like the tree itself, it resists fire and attack from insects. Therefore, it is valuable for construction,

A giant sequoia of the Pacific Forest in California.

house shingles, railroad ties, and electric light poles. Shingles made of redwood can last 40 years. However, one drawback in working redwood is that it requires a long and difficult process to dry it thoroughly.

Full-scale cutting of redwoods began about 1850, and by today hundreds of thousands of acres have been cut over. Yet, many groves of redwoods and sequoias have been preserved and these trees are probably not now in danger of extinction.

As may be imagined, cutting down one of these giant conifers is an awesome task. The lumbermen must be very skillful and experienced. Their aim is to have the tree fall unbroken in a chosen spot.

First, a platform is built around the trunk, about eight feet from the ground. Two men saw through one side of the tree almost to the center. Another cut is made on the opposite side, about two feet above the first one and almost to the center. Woodsmen with axes climb the platform and chop out the solid wood between the two cuts. Done correctly, the mighty tree falls where it is supposed to, and all in one piece.

Next come the "ringers" and "peelers." They cut a ring around the tree about every 14 feet and peel the bark away. Soon there are great piles of bark and branches scattered around the trunk. To dispose of this debris, the lumbermen choose a windless, foggy day and make a huge fire. The actual tree trunk itself may be charred by the intense heat of the flames. However, the woodsmen first plug any openings in the trunk with clay to be sure that it doesn't catch fire.

One of the largest of the big trees was cut down in 1853. It was over 300 feet tall. After the 18-inch-thick bark had been removed, the solid wood measured 25 feet in diameter. The stump, on which more than 40 people could stand, was used as a dance floor.

The estimated volume of lumber in this California Ponderosa pine is 20,000 board feet.

A totally different American woodland is found in the Petrified Forest National Park in eastern Arizona. Petrified forests are the stonelike remains of trees that grew millions of years ago. Instead of simply decaying, the trees were buried in mud that contained volcanic ash. Ash from volcanoes has large amounts of iron, silica, and manganese. These minerals entered the wood, preserving it and turning it to stone. Millions of years later the remains were uncovered, mostly by erosion.

The Petrified Forest in Arizona is particularly beautiful because the iron and manganese in the ash have produced brilliant colors in the wood.

The first chief of the U.S. Forest Service gives his name to the Gifford Pinchot National Forest in Washington.

THE U. S. FOREST SERVICE

In 1905 the forest reserves of the Department of the Interior were transferred to the Department of Agriculture and the U. S. Forest Service was created, with Gifford Pinchot (1865–1946) as its first chief. Pinchot had studied forestry in Europe and later taught it at Yale University. *Forestry* means the managing of forests to preserve them and to keep them producing the goods that man needs.

Pinchot brought the word "conservation" to the nation's attention. He said: "Conservation is the farsighted utilization, preservation, and/or renewal of forests, waters, lands, and minerals, for the greatest good of the greatest number for the longest time." Conservation became the first aim of the Forest Service.

The U. S. Forest Service has three major activities: to manage national forests and national grasslands; to help state, local, and private forest owners with forest management; and to carry out research in forest conservation and use.

Managing our national forests and grasslands is a huge job in itself. In 1891 and 1905 presidential proclamations declared certain public lands as national forests or grasslands. Today there are 154 national forests and 19 national grasslands. Together they cover almost 187 million acres.

The Forest Service follows what it calls a "multiple use"

idea in managing the national lands. This idea recognizes five main benefits that people get from the forests: timber, water, forage, wildlife, and recreation. The Forest Service works in all five areas.

Under Forest Service supervision, private companies cut trees for the timber that the country and the world needs. About 12 million board feet of wood a year comes from our national forests, or about one-fourth of all the timber harvested in the United States annually. Money from the sale of the timber goes to the United States Treasury, except for a certain percentage, which is spent on schools and roads where the national forests are located.

Pure water is needed by people, by agriculture, and by industry. A good deal of the water supply in the United States flows through national forest land. The Forest Service works to control floods and to prevent erosion, the wearing away of the soil. It manages watersheds, areas into which a river drains or which catch and hold the waters of a river system. The service also gives "first-aid" treatment to burned-out lands in order to keep the water supply safe.

Cattle and sheep are allowed to graze on ranges in the national forests and also on the grasslands. Some 20,000 cattle owners, mostly with small herds, hold grazing permits, for which they are charged a fee.

The Forest Service tries to see that animals and fish are available in the forests for hunters and fishermen, but it also wants to keep the wildlife in balance with available food and shelter. Both hunting and fishing in the national forests are under state laws.

Millions and millions of Americans enjoy the national forests each year. The Forest Service maintains campgrounds, picnic areas, winter sports sites, swimming sites, boating areas, and trails for recreation.

Critics of the multiple use idea contend that, in fact, it does not really work very well because there are too many interests competing for the use of the forests. It is true that over the years, even with the best of intentions, our national timber and other resources have suffered much abuse. Today many government leaders argue that we are depleting our resources by cutting too much timber.

Besides managing public lands, the Forest Service helps state and local governments and private owners to manage over 500 million acres of forests and watershed areas. It gives aid in protecting forests from disease — 26 states take part in the Forest Pest Control Act — and in reforesting land — 46 states cooperate with the Forest Service in the Tree Seedling Program. In 1969, for instance, about 700 million trees were grown in state-owned nurseries, to be planted on more than one million acres. The Forest Service also provides technical and financial assistance to the Cooperative Forest Fire Control Program, to which all 50 states belong.

About one-third of the fire prevention and control work in the United States is handled by the Forest Service. The states, with aid from the federal government, do almost all the rest. There are also some private associations devoted to fire prevention and control.

Despite warnings to the public, fire watches, and fire prevention practices, an average of 125,000 forest fires occur in the United States each year. People cause about 95 percent of them. Thousands of acres of healthy forests are lost through carelessness — a cigarette tossed from a car or a campfire left to smolder. Lightning is blamed for the remaining 5 percent of forest fires. The figures vary, however, in different parts of the country. Lightning causes only 2 percent of the forest fires in the southern states and as high as 70 percent in the Rocky Mountain area.

Aerial view of a forest fire in the Coconino National Forest in Arizona.

Since people are responsible for so many fires, the Forest Service tries to keep the public informed about the dangers of fire. Most everyone is familiar with Smokey the Bear. He appears on posters and television, asking people not to be careless with fire in the forests.

There are three types of forest fires: ground, crown, and surface. A *ground fire* burns the material that is under the surface debris — such as leaves and plant life — on the forest floor. A *crown fire* rages from treetop to treetop. A *surface fire*, the most common type, burns the surface debris itself.

Sometimes fires can be prevented by knowing where they are likely to start. In a dry season, a so-called high-risk area may be a forest that has a lot of debris, including dead trees, on the forest floor. Under safe conditions, this material can be

The result of a 20,000 acre fire that swept along the shore of a lake in Canada.

burned, thereby reducing the danger of a spreading forest fire. Firebreaks are sometimes built in high-risk areas. These are strips of land that have been cleared of all debris. The theory is that the fire will reach the firebreak and not be able to jump across it, thereby stopping the spread of the fire.

If a fire cannot be prevented, the next best thing is to spot it as soon as possible. Forest fire detection is a big part of the work of the U. S. Forest Service and other organizations.

Forest fire detection is not a new idea in the United States. Colonial settlers as well as Indians kept a lookout for forest fires. They were not particularly interested in saving the forests, but in saving their own lives and property. Early in their history, states such as Massachusetts and New Jersey passed laws concerning forest fires. But it was really not until the beginning of the twentieth century that the country had any sort of forest fire detection program. It was mostly carried out by private-property owners. Finally, in 1911, under the so-called Weeks law, the federal government began to cooperate with the states in protecting forests from fire.

One of the earliest ways of detecting forest fires was the use of the lookout tower. The first ones were just platforms mounted high in trees. Later, permanent wooden stations were built, equipped with telephones. Still later, steel towers were used, many containing living quarters for the fire watchers.

By 1953 there were over 5,000 lookout towers in the United States. Since that time the number in operation has been steadily declining. The reason is due to the use of the airplane.

In 1945 four state-owned airplanes were being used for fire detection. Some 20 years later the number had reached 200. About the same number of privately owned planes were hired.

There are advantages and disadvantages to both the lookout tower and the airplane.

In the lookout tower, someone can be watching for fires 24 hours a day, in any kind of weather, including high winds when a plane might not be able to fly. Radio communication is generally more reliable from the tower than from a plane. But the cost of manning these towers has become very expensive. An even greater disadvantage is the so-called blind area. A lookout in a tower cannot spot a fire quickly if it starts on land that is hidden behind a high mountain, for example. The airplane can. The plane also allows the spotter to give more detailed information about the fire than could the guard in a lookout tower.

The disadvantages of aerial detection are the hazards of weather and the fact that planes cannot provide a continuous watch. They cannot be in the air all of the time.

In a fire-fighting demonstration for forestry personnel, a helicopter drops 160 gallons of water.

The U. S. Forest Service, in its Northern Forest Fire Laboratory, is constantly conducting research in fire detection. The ideal system, toward which the researchers are working, would be one in which fires would be detected the instant they start; which would operate as well in the darkness as in light or in any kind of bad weather; and which would also be reliable and inexpensive.

55

To conduct research in forest conservation, the Forest Service has eight regional Experiment Stations, a Forest Products Laboratory in Madison, Wisconsin, and an Institute of Tropical Forestry in Puerto Rico. There scientists study how to protect forests from pests and fire; how to grow and harvest healthier trees; and how better to use the products of the forest. They look for new uses for timber and devise better guides to recreation areas, among many other research projects.

There are some 49 forestry schools in the United States, all part of a university or college, where a student may prepare for a career in forestry. Most of the schools are approved by the Society of American Foresters, which rates the kind of instruction and the qualifications of the instructors. A typical example might be the School of Forestry and Conservation at the University of California in Berkeley. There a student may earn a Bachelor of Science degree, with a major in forestry, wood science, or technology. He may study forest management, range management, wildlife habitat management, industrial forestry, and park and recreational land management. After his sophomore year he spends ten weeks of summer camp in the Sierra Nevada forest. The school provides six experimental forests and field stations nearby for further study.

ECOLOGY AND CONSERVATION

Ecology has become an important word in our modern world. It means the study of living things in relation to where they live, or to their environment. The word actually comes from two Greek words that mean "the study of the home."

The forest home, or community, can be divided into five different levels. Each level houses different plants and animals. The bottom level is the *floor* of the forest. Piles of branches, leaves, flower petals, and animal refuse cover the ground and are turned into humus (material formed by the decay of animal and vegetable matter) by fungi, earthworms, ants, and bacteria in the soil.

The second level is the *herb layer*. This is the home of snakes and toads, mice and insects. They dart about among the soft-stemmed green plants and low wild flowers and mosses.

Above the herb layer is the *shrub layer*. Here are woody plants that shelter small animals, as well as many birds, which eat the seeds and berries of the shrubs.

The fourth level is called the *understudy*. Made up of small trees, it is also filled with birds and animals that use the trees as nesting sites.

The fifth level in the forest is the *canopy*, formed by the tops of the tallest trees. If the trees are close together, not

The Kaibab forest, almost destroyed when man tampered with its ecology.

much sunlight gets through to the lower levels. The more sunlight, the greater the number of plants and animals in the forest. The canopy level may be occupied by eagles and other birds, squirrels, spiders, and thousands of insects that feed on the tree leaves.

In a healthy woodland, all levels exist together, growing, multiplying, dieing, being replaced. When something happens to change one part of this complex coexistence, the entire forest may undergo a change, serious enough to destroy it.

A classic example of what can happen when man tampers with the ecology of a woodland is the story of the Kaibab forest of northern Arizona. Before 1907 the Kaibab forest was, in the words of a visitor, "the most enchanting region it has ever been our privilege to visit." Douglas fir, ponderosa pine, and Engelmann spruce covered 700,000 acres of this enchanted land. For hundreds of years Indians had hunted the mule deer in this region, which was also home to wolves, mountain lions, and coyotes.

It is said that about 4,000 deer roamed the Kaibab forest in 1906 when the federal government declared the woodland a national game reserve. For the next 25 years, in order to build up the deer population, deer hunting was forbidden, and mountain lions, coyotes, and wolves — the deers' enemies — were hunted down and killed, over 6,000 of them.

The program was fantastically successful. By 1925 about 100,000 deer roamed in the shade of the tall pines and spruce.

Unfortunately, the program was *too* successful. And too late it was realized that the Kaibab forest simply could not feed 100,000 deer. Having eaten every plant and shrub within reach, the deer began to starve. More than half of them starved to death by 1926.

Sad as the fate of the mule deer was, they were not alone. The deer had eaten just about everything in the forest, stripping it bare like a band of locusts. Some plant life, such as raspberry bushes and willow trees, simply never grew again in the Kaibab.

Hunting was permitted once more, and by 1942 the mule deer herd numbered about 8,000. But because many of the plants the deer usually ate had disappeared, the remaining

59

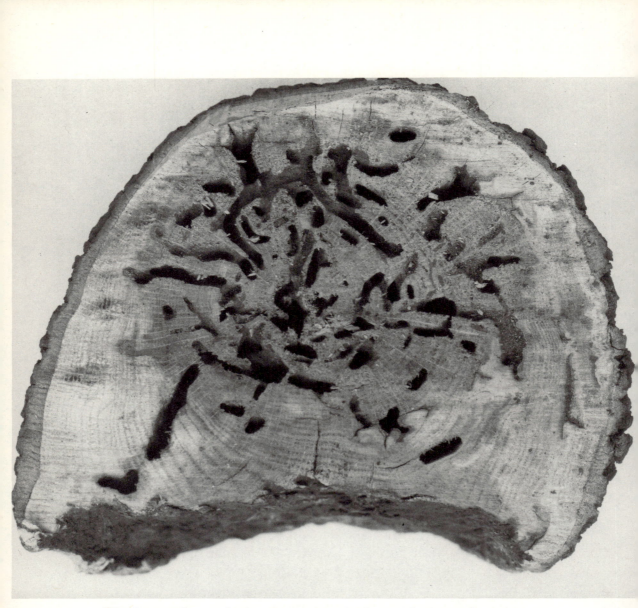

The destructive work of carpenter ants in the trunk of an oak.

deer were generally sickly and ill-fed. So many trees had been thinned out that certain grasses grew in their place. The ecology of the Kaibab forest had been changed; it would never be the same again.

The lesson of the Kaibab forest is that man must work *with* the laws of nature, not against them.

Sometimes it is not man that breaks the delicate balance of nature. This is illustrated by what happened in Colorado, in a forest of Engelmann spruce trees, over 20 years ago. A member of the forest community was the bark beetle, a fly-sized insect that fed upon old spruce trees. Eaten by woodpeckers and other insects, the beetle population was kept in check. There were not enough of them to attack the young trees, and the damage they did to the old ones actually aided the forest because the old trees died quicker, leaving space for new growth.

Then came a heavy windstorm. The roots of spruce trees are not buried deep in the soil, and many trees were uprooted. The beetles had a feast, hidden from the woodpeckers in the tangle of fallen branches. As a result, the number of beetles grew and grew. So great was their number that they were able to destroy young trees, too. In about six years, the Engelmann spruce forest was nearly destroyed. Its ecology had been changed.

Of course, there are things that man can do to improve a forest without damaging its natural existence. Man must first understand the ecology of the forest. Then he must work with it.

Before the seventeenth century, over one billion acres of trees covered the land that would later become the United States. By 1850, 900 million acres were in forest. The population was over 23 million, and the demands for lumber were steadily growing. By 1900 the population was 76 million. A

61

Logging in southeastern Alaska.

great deal of the pine forests of the lake states had already been cleared. About 800 million acres of forest remained. By 1938 the figure was 771 million acres. By 1945 it had dropped to 765 million. But by 1960, 773 million acres were in forest. The decline of the American forest was being stopped.

What caused the decline? And how is it being reversed?

When the first settlers arrived in the New World, trees were everywhere. Wood was needed, and it was free. No one gave much thought to how long the supply would last.

One man who did was William Penn (1644–1718), founder of the colony of Pennsylvania in 1681. Penn declared that for every five acres cleared in his colony, one acre must be left in forest. But William Penn was very much the exception.

By 1800 the eastern part of the young United States was already experiencing a shortage of wood. So much forest had been cleared for farming, so much wood had been cut for building and fuel that the lumber industry began to look westward.

The decline continued as trees fell before the march of settlers to the West. The Civil War in the 1860's brought heavy demands for wood, and much forest land was destroyed in the fighting. By the 1890's many of the forests in the Midwest had been cleared. The loggers moved south and then farther west.

The lumber industry had chopped its way to the Pacific by the time Theodore Roosevelt became president in 1901. He set up a committee to investigate what was happening to the country's natural resources. The report was shocking. The reckless cutting of trees, which left the land bare and unprotected, was causing great areas of erosion. Without protection from trees, the soil was being washed away by streams and blown away by wind. Bad logging practices wasted about one-fourth of the timber cut. The debris, which the loggers carelessly left behind them, became the fuel for rampaging forest fires. Clearly something had to be done.

Roosevelt had already found the man to do it. Heading the conservation committee was Gifford Pinchot. Through his efforts studies were made of the country's woodlands to determine how they could best be managed and preserved. Schools of forestry were started, national forest land increased, and fire control practices put into effect.

Yet, the decline of the American forest marched on. Demands for wood products during World War I plunged the forest reserves to an all-time low. The decline was briefly stopped during the depression of the 1930's when the need for wood products dwindled. In 1938 the federally sponsored Civilian Conservation Corps planted over two billion young trees.

The 1940's and World War II brought another heavy call for wood. During this period, 10 percent of the timber supply

63

came from the North, 35 percent from the South, and 55 percent from the West.

It was not until 1960 that the decline of the American forest seemed to have been stopped at last. For the first time, the amount of new wood grown in the United States equaled the amount of wood cut. This was largely brought about by expanded and dedicated conservation practices by both the federal and state governments and private lumber companies.

Through the years the federal government had made some efforts to save America's forests. In 1831 the cutting of trees on federally owned land was forbidden. In 1873 the Timber Culture Act was passed. It offered free land to settlers who would plant 40 acres of trees for every 160 acres given. The year before, the first national park in the world had been established at Yellowstone, in Wyoming, Montana, and Idaho. (Now, 90 other countries have national park systems.) In 1911 a law was passed to protect the watersheds of navigable rivers. The Clarke-McNary Act of 1918 provided for fire control in federal forests. At that time about 40 million acres of trees were lost through fire each year. In 1964 the National Wilderness Preservation System was created. It assured that over nine million acres of wilderness areas would be left in their natural state for all to enjoy. These and other acts by the federal government have aided the fight to save our national forests.

Better trained and more conservation-minded lumbermen have also played an important role in the fight. Many modern lumbermen look upon trees not merely as commercial timber but also as a crop that must be carefully planted, tended, and harvested. They carry a textbook instead of an ax. They

An experimental pine woodland in Alabama.

65

develop better trees, find better ways of fighting plant diseases, reseed cut-over areas, and try to restore the damage done by fire.

Today's foresters fight to save our wooded areas in three main ways: they make better, more complete use of each tree cut; they improve the forests by better harvesting and reseeding methods; and they seek to reduce losses due to fire and disease.

So, it would seem that the decline of the American forest has stopped. But unfortunately, that is not enough. It is said that the United States will double its need for wood by the year 2000. If that is so, we must do more than merely grow as much wood as we cut. We must find new and better ways to produce more wood on the land we now have.

WOODLANDS AND INDUSTRY

Americans use wood — lots of it. About 80 percent of all the houses in the United States have wooden frames. An average house contains about 13,000 board feet of timber in one form or another. Every year each man, woman, and child in the United States uses an average of over 560 pounds of paper.

Wood has always been one of man's most necessary materials. He used it to keep warm and to heat his food. He needed it for shelter and for ships to travel and explore his world. He built bridges of wood and airplanes with wooden frames. Trees gave him shade, as well as fruits and nuts.

Today there are many other materials for use as fuel or in construction. Yet, our need for wood keeps increasing.

Trees provide us with an almost endless list of wood products — more than 5,000 come from North American forests alone. Lumber is needed for furniture, boats, musical instruments, matches, house and truck trailers, brooms, tools, toys, and sporting goods, to name just a few. Wood is used in telephone poles, fence posts, and railroad ties, in dock pilings and barrels. Naval stores, the trade name for rosin and turpentine, come from wood, mainly the southern pines. Trees provide maple sugar and syrup. And trees produce nuts and fruits, as well as vegetable oils. Over 40 million Christmas trees are used each year in the United States.

The three largest uses for wood in the United States are in building construction of one form or another, in wood chemical products, and as heating and cooking fuels.

Besides frames for houses, wood is used in flooring and paneling, as well as in all kinds of furniture. Veneer and plywood are important, too. Veneer is a thin sheet of wood "peeled" off the log with a long blade. It is often glued onto furniture as decoration. Plywood is made by gluing sheets of veneer together in a kind of sandwich. It is widely used for shelves and in house repairs.

Woods that have been converted into fibers and plastics are known as wood chemical products. They include paper, almost entirely made from wood pulp, for use in books, newspapers, and all sorts of writing and packing materials. Some other wood chemical products are rayon, a fiber made from wood pulp; cellophane and cellophane tape; and plastic toys and household utensils.

Since trees differ widely from one another, their uses differ, too. Hardwood trees are usually preferred for making furniture; the softwoods are often used in paper products and construction. The use of a particular wood may depend on its toughness, weight, lack of knots, tendency to swell or shrink, and other factors. For instance, the wood of the white ash is stiff, but it bends well and easily wears smooth. Therefore, it is ideal for baseball bats and tennis rackets. The wood of the red spruce is light but strong. It is good for canoe paddles and ladder rungs. The hard tough wood of the hickory makes it desirable for tool handles and skis.

The forest products industry owns about 13 percent of the commercial forests in the United States. Yet, it produces about one-third of all the timber needed for wood products. This is because the industry's land is managed especially to increase the tree yield.

A worker at a tree nursery inspects his pine saplings.

Today's foresters use four main methods for harvesting trees. They are designed to keep the forests healthy and to make them more productive. The methods are called clear cutting, selective cutting, the seed-tree system, and the shelterwood system.

Clear cutting is often used where the trees are all about the same age. Areas of differing sizes are cut down, leaving blocks of trees standing in-between. The cut sections are re-seeded either by airplane or by hand, or naturally from seeds that blow off the remaining trees. This method is often used in harvesting such trees as Douglas fir and black spruce, for they reproduce easily in direct sunlight. It takes about 40 years for the new stand of trees to produce seeds. Clear cutting will result in fairly even stands of trees, but there are some hazards from wind and water erosion on the newly cut land.

The *selective cutting* method may be used in a forest containing trees that grow well in shade. Young red spruce trees, for instance, grow well in the shade of older and larger trees. When the young trees mature, the older trees are cut. New trees will grow in the shade of the now mature red spruces.

In the *seed-tree system*, perhaps five or six healthy and mature trees are left on each acre when the rest are cut down. The remaining trees reseed the land for a period of five to ten years. Then they are cut, too. This method works well in a woodland of relatively fast-growing trees, such as the southern pines. They may be ready to harvest 30 years after reseeding.

The *shelterwood system* allows trees to be cut at different states of growth. The first cutting removes unhealthy trees and gives more sunlight to the healthy ones. The second cutting removes about half of the remaining trees, leaving the strongest and most mature. These older trees protect the new seedlings from too much sun or bad weather. When the young trees no longer need their protection, the older trees are cut.

70

No matter how carefully and scientifically forests are managed, the fact remains that trees take a long time to grow. For instance, if a Douglas fir tree was planted in 1970, it may be usable for a Christmas tree by 1978 or 1980. By the year 2010 it could be cut as pulpwood, to be made into paper. By 2030, when it may be 100 feet tall, the tree could be used as a telephone pole. In 2070 it might make good timber or plywood.

To fill our needs for wood, modern foresters are trying to "hurry up" a tree's growing process. Hybrid trees are grown at tree nurseries around the country. They are created by crossing certain types of plants that have desirable features. The result can be trees that grow faster and larger and have greater resistance to disease. The hybrids are planted in nursery beds where they are carefully tended under almost ideal conditions. The "superseeds" of the hybrid can be collected mechanically, chemically treated to resist disease, and then sown by helicopter.

Another way in which the forest industry tries to meet the demand for more timber is by better use of each log. In 1900 about one-third of a tree ended up as a product. Today almost three-fourths of the tree does. Better saws reduce waste. The bark may be made into valuable products. Machines called chippers make once-useless pieces of wood into pulp for paper. (The illustration on page 72 shows how a tree is cut for the best use.)

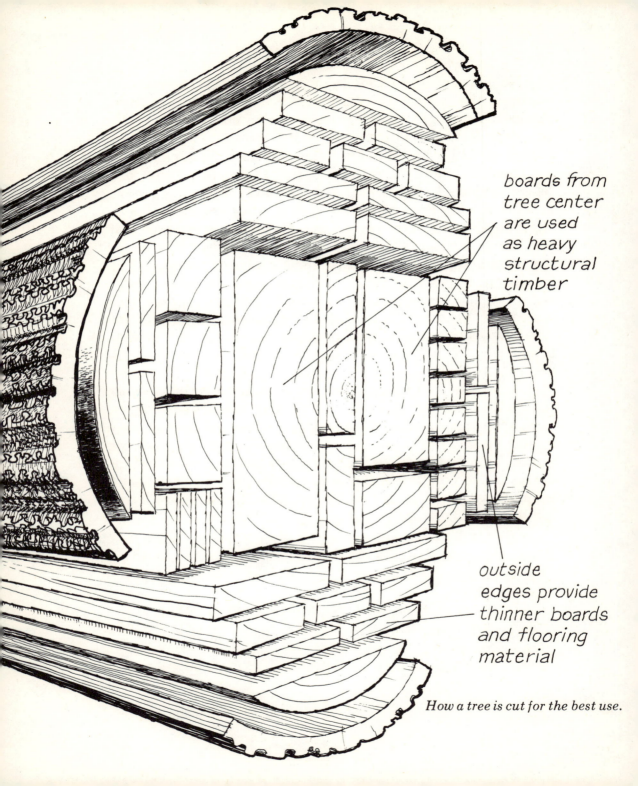

boards from
tree center
are used
as heavy
structural
timber

outside
edges provide
thinner boards
and flooring
material

How a tree is cut for the best use.

WHERE TO SEE OUR NATIONAL FORESTS

The 153 national forests in the United States, and the one in Puerto Rico, are spread over more than 182 million acres. (The map on page 81 shows their locations.) Depending on their size and where they are located, the national forests offer many different kinds of recreation to the visitor. All of them offer beautiful scenery.

Some 7,700 developed campgrounds and picnic grounds can be found in our national forests, as well as 80,000 miles of streams and rivers and some of the best trout waters in the country. About 180 ski areas and more than 400 resorts are on national forest land. There are 112,000 miles of riding and hiking trails; 115,000 miles of roads; and nearly 15 million acres of what are called wildernesses, or primitive areas, where the only way to travel is by foot, canoe, or horseback. Some of the national forests charge a fee per automobile to enter.

Listed below are the national forests. You may locate them by number on the map. For more information, write to the headquarters of the Forest Supervisors in the towns shown in parentheses.

Key: B = boating; C = camping; F = fishing; H = hiking; Hb = horseback riding; P = picnicking; R = resort (cabins or hotels) areas, S = swimming, W = winter sports areas. An * means that the forest contains a wilderness area.

Alabama:	1. William B. Bankhead Natl. Forest (Montgomery), 178,739 acres, CFPS
	2. Conechu (Montgomery), 83,900, CFPS
	3. Talladega (Montgomery), 357,470, CFPRS
	4. Tuskegee (Montgomery), 10,777, FP

Alabama:
1. William B. Bankhead Natl. Forest (Montgomery), 178,739 acres, CFPS
2. Conechu (Montgomery), 83,900, CFPS
3. Talladega (Montgomery), 357,470, CFPRS
4. Tuskegee (Montgomery), 10,777, FP

Alaska:
1. Chugach Natl. Forest (Anchorage), 4,723,397 acres, CFPSW
2. Tongass — North Division (Juneau), 16,011,-643 (both divisions), BFHPSW
3. Tongass — South Division (Ketchikan), BCFPSW

Arizona:
1. Apache Natl. Forest* (Springerville), 1,806,751 acres — partly in N.M. — BCFHHbPR
2. Coconino* (Flagstaff), 1,808,043, BCFHbPRW
3. Coronado* (Tucson), 1,721,547 — partly in N.M. — CFHHbPRSW
4. Kaibab* (Williams), 1,727,995, CFHbPR
5. Prescott* (Prescott), 1,247,834, CFHbPR
6. Sitgreaves (Holbrook), 795,504, CHHbPRS
7. Tonto* (Phoenix), 2,890,853, BCFHHbPRS

Arkansas:
1. Ouachita Natl. Forest (Hot Springs), 1,563,383 acres — partly in Okla. — CFHPRS
2. Ozark (Russellville), 1,088,164, CFPRS

California:
1. Angeles Natl. Forest* (Pasadena), 648,866 acres, BCFHHbPRSW
2. Cleveland* (San Diego), 393,085, CFPR
3. Eldorado* (Placerville), 652,567, BCFHbPRSW
4. Inyo* (Bishop), 1,835,960 — partly in Nev. — BCFHPRSW
5. Klamath* (Yreka), 1,696,965 — partly in Oreg. — CFHHbPR
6. Lassen* (Susanville), 1,045,624, BCFHHbPRSW
7. Los Padres* (Santa Barbara), 1,724,108, CFHPRSW

8. Mendocino* (Willows), 872,237, CFHHbPR
9. Modoc* (Alturas), 1,689,508, CFPRSW
10. Plumas (Quincy), 1,146,723, BCFPRW
11. San Bernardino* (San Bernardino), 616,315, CFHbPRSW
12. Sequoia* (Porterville), 1,115,858, BCFHHbPRSW
13. Shasta-Trinity* (Redding), 2,066,254 (two forests), BCFHbPRSW
14. Sierra* (Fresno), 1,293,180, BCFHHbPRSW
15. Six Rivers (Eureka), 939,399, CFHbRW
16. Stanislaus* (Sonora), 896,312, BCFHHbPRSW
17. Tahoe (Nevada City), 696,536, BCFHHbPRSW

Colorado:

1. Arapaho Natl. Forest* (Golden), 1,003,373 acres, CFHHbPRW
2. Grand Mesa-Uncompahgre* (Delta), 1,317,964 (two forests), CFHbPRW
3. Gunnison* (Gunnison), 1,662,860, CFHbPRW
4. Pike (Colorado Springs), 1,106,101, CFPRW
5. Rio Grande* (Monte Vista), 1,799,389, CFHHb-RW
6. Roosevelt* (Fort Collins), 776,139, BCFHHbPRW
7. Routt* (Steamboat Springs), 1,125,045, CFH-HbPRW
8. San Isabel (Pueblo), 1,106,510, CFHHbPRW
9. San Juan* (Durango), 1,850,405, CFHHbPRW
10. White River* (Glenwood Springs), 1,960,183, CFHHbPRW

Florida:

1. Apalachicola Natl. Forest (Tallahassee), 556,-972 acres, BCFPS
2. Ocala* (Tallahassee), 361,497, CFPS
3. Osceola (Tallahassee), 157,233, BCFPS

Georgia:

1. Chattahoochee Natl. Forest (Gainesville), 680,-618 acres, BCFHPS
2. Oconee (Gainesville), 102,911, CFP

75

Idaho:

1. Boise Natl. Forest* (Boise), 2,632,321 acres, BCFPRSW
2. Caribou (Pocatello), 971,781 — partly in Utah and Wyo. — CFHbPRW
3. Challis* (Challis), 2,447,243, BCFHHbPR
4. Clearwater* (Orofino), 1,675,562, CFHPR
5. Coeur d'Alene (Coeur d'Alene), 723,168, CFPRW
6. Kaniksu* (Sandpoint), 1,621,898 — partly in Mont. and Wash. — BCFPRSW
7. Nezperce* (Grangeville), 2,198,094, CFHHbPR
8. Payette* (McCall), 2,307,158, CFHW
9. Salmon* (Salmon), 1,767,585, BCFPR
10. St. Joe (St. Maries), 862,018, CFPRSW
11. Sawtooth* (Twin Falls), 1,803,164 — partly in Utah — CFHHbPRSW
12. Targhee (St. Anthony), 1,663,363 — partly in Wyo. — CFHHbPRW

Illinois:

1. Shawnee Natl. Forest (Harrisburg), 217,982 acres, BCFPRS

Indiana:

1. Hoosier Natl. Forest (Bedford), 134,779 acres, CFPRS

Kentucky:

1. Daniel Boone Natl. Forest (Winchester), 464,-683 acres, CFPRS

Louisiana:

1. Kisatchie Natl. Forest (Alexandria), 593,064 acres, BCFPS

Michigan:

1. Huron Natl. Forest (Cadillac), 415,493 acres, CFPRSW
2. Manistee (Cadillac), 465,140, BCFPRSW
3. Ottawa (Ironwood), 886,484, CFPRS
4. Hiawatha (Escanaba), 839,960 (two separate sections), BCFPRSW

Minnesota:	1. Chippewa Natl. Forest (Cass Lake), 644,602 acres, BCFPRSW
	2. Superior* (Duluth), 2,040,569, BCFPRW
Mississippi:	1. Bienville Natl. Forest (Jackson), 175,697 acres, CFPS
	2. Delta (Jackson), 58,923, CFP
	3. DeSoto (Jackson), 501,548, BCFPRS
	4. Holly Springs (Jackson), 143,729, CPS
	5. Homochitto (Jackson), 189,053, CFPS
	6. Tombigbee (Jackson), 65,254, BCFPS
Missouri:	1. Clark Natl. Forest (Rolla), 768,254 acres, CFP
	2. Mark Twain (Springfield), 608,719, CFRS
Montana:	1. Beaverhead Natl. Forest* (Dillon), 2,111,070 acres, CFHPRW
	2. Bitterroot* (Hamilton), 1,575,919 — partly in Idaho — CFHHbPRW
	3. Custer* (Billings), 1,185,663 — partly in S. Dak. — CFHHbPRW
	4. Deerlodge* (Butte), 1,181,276, CFHHbPRW
	5. Flathead* (Kalispell), 2,341,664, BCFHHbPRSW
	6. Gallatin* (Bozeman), 1,701,338, CFHHbPRW
	7. Helena* (Helena), 969,000, CFHHbPRW
	8. Kootenai* (Libby), 1,819,545, — partly in Idaho — CFHbPRW
	9. Lewis and Clark* (Great Falls), 1,834,612, CFHHbPRW
	10. Lolo (Missoula), 2,086,234 — partly in Idaho — CFHHbPRSW
Nebraska:	1. Central Plains Forestry (Lincoln), 245,414 acres, CFP

Nevada:
1. Humboldt Natl. Forest* (Elko), 2,512,258 acres, CFHHbPRW
2. Toiyabe* (Reno), 3,119,593 — partly in Calif. — CFHHbPRSW

New Hampshire:
1. White Mountain Natl. Forest* (Laconia), 716,-157 acres — partly in Maine — CFHPRSW

New Mexico:
1. Carson Natl. Forest* (Taos), 1,419,732 acres, CFPW
2. Cibola (Albuquerque), 1,599,337, CFPRW
3. Gila* (Silver City), 2,694,447, CFHHbPR
4. Lincoln* (Alamogordo), 1,085,302, CFHHbPRW
5. Santa Fe* (Santa Fe), 1,440,511, CHHbPRW

North Carolina:
1. Croatan Natl. Forest (Asheville), 152,373 acres, BCFP
2. Nantahala (Asheville), 449,281, BCFHPS
3. Pisgah* (Asheville), 478,297, CFHHbPS
4. Uwharrie (Asheville), 43,571, F

Ohio:
1. Wayne Natl. Forest (Ironton and Athens ranger stations), 118,944 acres, CFPS

Oregon:
1. Deschutes Natl. Forest* (Bend), 1,587,690 acres, CFHHbPRSW
2. Fremont* (Lakeview), 1,208,302, BCPRW
3. Malheur* (John Day), 1,204,974, CFHHbPRW
4. Mount Hood* (Portland), 1,115,746, CFHHbPR-SW
5. Ochoco (Prineville), 845,855, BCFPR
6. Rogue River (Medford), 621,473 — partly in Calif. — CFHHbPRSW
7. Siskiyou* (Grants Pass), 1,081,006 — partly in Calif. — BCHHbPR
8. Siuslaw (Corvallis), 618,685, BCFPRS

9. Umatilla (Pendleton), 1,389,709 — partly in Wash. — BCFHHbPRW
10. Umpqua (Roseburg), 984,497, BCFHHbPRW
11. Wallowa-Whitman* (Baker), 2,497,094 (two natl. forests), CFHHbPRW
12. Willamette* (Eugene), 1,665,979, BCFHHbPRSW
13. Winema* (Klamath Falls), 908,984, BCFPRS

Pennsylvania:
1. Allegheny Natl. Forest (Warren), 475,749 acres, CFPRS

South Carolina:
1. Francis Marion Natl. Forest (Columbia), 245,-657 acres, BCFP
2. Sumter (Columbia), 342,082, CFPS

South Dakota:
1. Black Hills Natl. Forest (Custer), 1,221,441 acres — partly in Wyo. — BCFHHbPRSW

Tennessee:
1. Cherokee Natl. Forest (Cleveland), 600,437 acres, BCHPS

Texas:
1. Angelina Natl. Forest (Lufkin), 154,389 acres, CFPS
2. Davy Crockett (Lufkin), 161,556, CFPS
3. Sabine (Lufkin), 183,842, CFPS
4. Sam Houston (Lufkin), 158,235, CFPS

Utah:
1. Ashley Natl. Forest* (Vernal), 1,271,146 acres, CFHHbPRW
2. Cache (Logan), 673,035 — partly in Idaho — CFHHbPW
3. Dixie (Cedar City), 1,883,688, CFPRW
4. Fishlake (Richfield), 1,424,538, CFPR
5. Manti-La Sal (Price), 1,263,473 — partly in Colo. — CFHHbPW
6. Uinta (Provo), 794,686, CFHPRW
7. Wasatch* (Salt Lake City), 876,820 — partly in Wyo. — BCHHbPRSW

Vermont:	1. Green Mountain Natl. Forest (Rutland), 233,-463 acres, CFHHbPRSW
Virginia:	1. George Washington Natl. Forest (Harrisonburg), 1,018,221 acres — partly in W. Va. — CFHPS
	2. Jefferson (Roanoke), 565,712, CFPRS
Washington:	1. Colville Natl. Forest (Colville), 939,919 acres, CFPRSW
	2. Gifford Pinchot (Vancouver), 1,259,910, BCFH-HbPRW
	3. Mount Baker* (Bellingham), 1,818,182, BCFH-HbPRW
	4. Okanogan* (Okanogan), 1,520,448, BCFHHbP-RSW
	5. Olympic (Olympia), 621,756, BCFHHbPRS
	6. Snoqualmie* (Seattle), 1,211,901, BCFHHbPW
	7. Wenatchee* (Wenatchee), 1,731,076, BCHHbP-RW
West Virginia:	1. Monongahela Natl. Forest (Elkins), 808,898 acres, CFHbPRS
Wisconsin:	1. Chequamegon Natl. Forest (Park Falls), 831,-327 acres, BCFPRSW
	2. Nicolet (Rhinelander), 643,875, BCFPRSW
Wyoming:	1. Bighorn Natl. Forest* (Sheridan), 1,113,769 acres, CFHHbPRW
	2. Bridger* (Kemmerer), 1,700,029, CFHPRSW
	3. Medicine Bow (Laramie), 1,094,824, CFHHbPRW
	4. Shoshone* (Cody), 2,424,937, CFHHbPRW
	5. Teton* (Jackson), 1,700,820, CFPRSW
Puerto Rico:	1. Caribbean Natl. Forest (Rio Pedras), 27,889 acres, CHPS

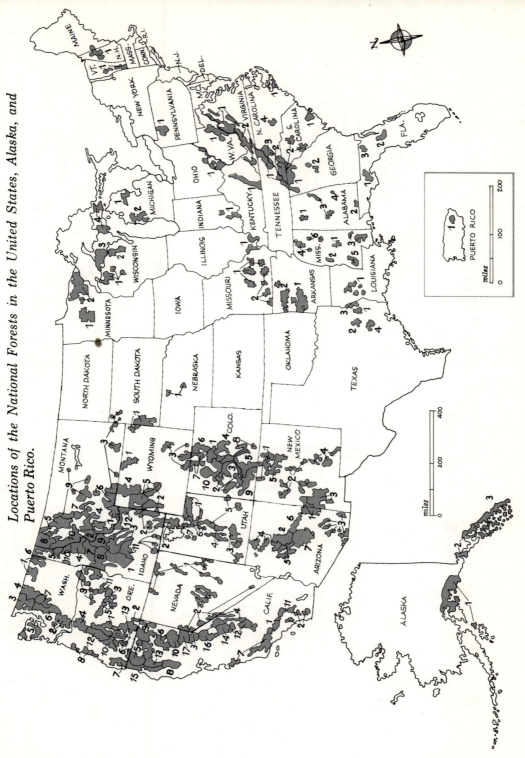

Locations of the National Forests in the United States, Alaska, and Puerto Rico.

FACTS ABOUT SOME MAJOR TREE TYPES IN THE UNITED STATES

Name	Type	Principal Location	Top height in feet (approx.)	Main Uses Today
1. Alder, Red	D(eciduous)	West	70	piling
2. Ash, White	D	East	100	athletic equipment
3. Aspen, Quaking	D	East, Rocky Mtns.	80	pulpwood (for paper), plywood
4. Beech, American	D	East	80	fuel, dams
5. Birch, Paper	D	East, Midwest	80	furniture, pulpwood
6. Cedar, Red	C(onifer)	East	100	chests, pencils
7. Cedar, White	C	East	75	shingles
8. Cherry	D	East to West	100	fruit
9. Chestnut, American (largely destroyed by blight)	D	East	60	rail fences, nuts
10. Cottonwood	D	East	150	lumber, pulpwood
11. Cypress, Bald	C	Southeast	120	lumber
12. Dogwood, Flowering	D	East, Central U.S.	40	tool handles, charcoal
13. Elm, American	D	East, Southeast	120	lumber
14. Fir, Balsam	C	Northeast	60	Christmas trees, pulpwood
15. Fir, Douglas	C	Pacific Coast, Rocky Mtns.	300	construction
16. Hemlock, Eastern	C	East	80	lumber, pulpwood
17. Hemlock, Western	C	West	180	lumber, pulpwood

18. Hickory	D	East, Southeast	70	athletic equipment
19. Holly, American	D	East	40	Christmas decorations
20. Juniper, Virginia	C	East, Midwest	100	fence posts
21. Larch, Western	C	West	150	lumber
22. Locust, Black	D	Midwest	75	shipbuilding, furniture
23. Maple, Sugar	D	East, Midwest, Southeast	120	syrup, sugar, furniture
24. Mulberry, Red	D	East, Central U.S.	60	fence posts, furniture
25. Oak, White	D	East	100	floors, furniture
26. Pecan	D	Central, South-central U.S.	100	nuts, boxes, crates
27. Persimmon	D	East, South, Midwest	50	fruit, honey
28. Pine, Eastern White	C	Northeast	100	furniture
29. Pine, Longleaf	C	South	100	naval stores
30. Pine, Ponderosa	C	Rocky Mtns.	200	construction
31. Poplar, Eastern cottonwood	D	East, Midwest	100	boxes, crates
32. Redwood	C	West Coast	350	lumber
33. Sassafras	D	East	100	fence posts, rails
34. Sequoia, Giant	C	West Coast	275	lumber
35. Spruce, White	C	Northeast	70	pulpwood
36. Sweet gum	D	East, Southeast	120	furniture
37. Sycamore, American	D	East, Midwest	100	lumber
38. Tulip tree (yellow poplar)	D	East, Southeast	150	furniture, pulpwood
39. Walnut, Black	D	East, Midwest	100	nuts, furniture
40. Willow, Black	D	East	100	artificial limbs, furniture

83

GLOSSARY OF WOODLAND TERMS

Angiosperm — seeds carried in a container.

Annual rings — circles inside tree trunk that tell age of a tree.

Bark — outside, visible layer of tree trunk that protects tree from weather, insects, and disease.

Blight — general term for any disease that attacks plant tissue.

Board foot — standard lumber measurement, 12 inches by 12 inches by 1 inch.

Cambium — living-tissue layer of tree trunk that produces annual rings.

Central Forest — hardwood forest stretching across northern United States and south to Texas.

Chippers — machines that convert small pieces of wood into pulp for making paper.

Chlorophyll — green coloring matter in leaves.

Conifers — softwood, usually evergreen trees with needlelike leaves.

Deciduous — hardwood, generally broad-leafed trees that usually shed their leaves each year.

Forest Service — part of Department of Agriculture concerned with managing woodlands.

Forestry — science of managing and preserving woodlands.

Gymnosperm — seeds without a protective covering.

Heartwood — dark dead center of tree trunk.

National forest — land set aside and preserved for public use and enjoyment.

Northern Forest — coniferous woodland stretching from Alaska to Appalachia.

Pacific Forest — coniferous woodland along western coast from Alaska to California, noted for redwoods and giant sequoias.

Palmate leaf — leaf with veins that branch out from the stem.

Parallel leaf — leaf with unusual parallel vein structure, as in leaves of the ginkgo tree.

Petrified Forest — woodland preserved and turned to stone by volcanic ash.

Phloem — tree trunk layer inside bark that carries food from leaves to roots.

Photosynthesis — process by which plant life consumes carbon dioxide and releases oxygen into the air.

Pinnate leaf — leaf with one center vein and smaller veins branching off it.

Plywood — sheets of veneer glued together and used as building material.

Rocky Mountain Forest — western woodland of huge timber trees.

Root system — usually underground part of tree that anchors trunk to the soil and absorbs water and minerals.

Sap — water and dissolved minerals in tree.

Sapwood — layer of tree trunk that carries sap throughout tree.

Selva — tropical rain forest in South America.

Southern Forest — southeastern woodland of pine and hardwoods.

Taiga — open woodlands in northern Asia characterized by mostly spruce and fir trees.

Taproot — long main underground tree root that may have hundreds of other roots growing from it.

Tropical Forest — smallest woodland zone in United States, found in Florida and Texas.

Veneer — thin sheet of wood "peeled" off log, used mainly in furniture decoration.

Wilderness areas — public lands left in natural primitive state.

BOOKS FOR FURTHER READING

Anyone who wishes to read more about woodlands should find these books of interest.

Brockman, C. Frank. *Trees of North America*. New York: Golden Press, 1968.

Farb, Peter. *The Forest*. New York: Time-Life Books, 1969.

Fenton, Carroll L. and Dorothy C. Pallas. *Trees and Their World*. New York: John Day, 1957.

Harrison, William C. *Forest Fire Fighters and What They Do*. New York: Franklin Watts, Inc., 1962.

Ketchum, Richard M. *The Secret Life of the Forest*. New York: American Heritage, 1970.

Lemmon, R. S. *Trees*. New York: Garrard, 1960.

Pine, Tillie S. and Joseph Levine. *Trees and How We Use Them*. New York: McGraw-Hill, 1969.

Rich, Louise Dickinson. *We Took to the Woods*. New York: J. B. Lippincott Company, 1963.

INDEX

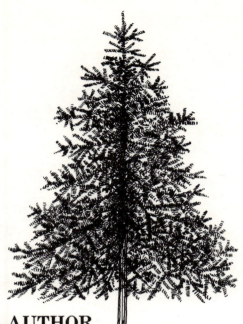

ABOUT THE AUTHOR

An editor of children's books at a New York publishing house, Corinne J. Naden served for four years in the U. S. Navy as a journalist. She was born in New York and now lives in Fort Lee, New Jersey. She was educated at the University of Wisconsin and New York University.

She is the author of *Grasslands Around the World*, the companion to this book, and a number of other children's books, including *The Chicago Fire*, *The Triangle Shirtwaist Fire*, *The Haymarket Affair*, *Frank Lloyd Wright*, *Golf*, *The Nile River*, *The First Book of Rivers*, *Let's Find Out About Frogs*, and *Let's Find Out About Bears*.